A SAILOR'S JOURNAL

IMPRESSIONS ALONG THE VOYAGE

Michael Warren

ISBN 979-8-88644-459-9 (Paperback)
ISBN 979-8-88644-460-5 (Digital)

Covenant Books
11661 Hwy 707
Murrells Inlet, SC 29576
www.covenantbooks.com

This book is dedicated to the memory of my mother Jackie Hawkins and my wife Elizabeth.

ACKNOWLEDGEMENTS

The insights gained along this leg of our lives' experiences were shared with many others. They include our family and friends all over the United States. On board were the faithful prayer warriors who joined in—especially those in our church family of LifePoint Church in Florissant, Missouri. Your vigil with us and consistent encouragement during the rough seas, long hours, and slow trek back to calm waters were an added anchor. You are loved and appreciated more than you can imagine.

Furthermore, you have inspired the chronicling of the thoughts contained within. It is my prayer that others may find peace, strength, and reassurance through the journal to follow and Christ is exalted.

A special thanks goes out to the editors, my daughter Aubrey and my beautiful wife Elizabeth.

Finally, I would like to honor my mother, Jackie Hawkins, who passed into her eternal celebration just after this manuscript was completed. Her short fight with illness and sudden passing is a further reminder that as life continues on this side of eternity, contending with stormy seas is a part of the journey.

CHAPTER 1

The Vessel of No One's Choosing

As Wednesday night begins to roll into Thursday morning, sleep is elusive. My mind is racing with a host of images of the past three days. Those images join a myriad of questions about what the hours ahead have in store. My emotions find themselves on a pendulum, swinging from a wave of gratitude to deep concern. They vacillate between warm feelings from the selfless reach of love and promised prayers to the chilling prospects of difficult roads yet to be traveled.

It is November of 2020. There are also the complications of this pandemic season that have made these past four days far more difficult to navigate. The hospital has limits—at a time when you so need openness. When you would cherish being joined by others, they are forbidden. When family wants to be present, they cannot. The moments tick by in anxious solitude. Ours is a vessel of no one's choosing.

This stormy season set sail Sunday morning—four days ago. It crashed in like a tsunami with a series of events that certainly altered the expected pattern of our lives. Liz, my dear bride of more than forty years, had been recovering from a fall while going up the basement steps. It had happened without fanfare over a month ago. The incident was not surprising. She has a tendency to be a bit clumsy. We laughed it off and assumed she would get over it in time.

Little was it realized that the fall had caused serious soft tissue damage to her hip, back, and leg. She was sore but thought nothing more of it. However, even with time, little progress had been made. She was tender and weakened. She had even stopped driving.

Normally, I open Sundays early, going to church to set things up in the worship center and get ready for the morning celebration. She then makes her way over—walking or driving depending on the weather—closer to service time. However, since her accident, I had been walking home and driving her to the church campus.

Then again this past week, I arrived home on Sunday morning to take her to church. As she headed out the door to come toward the car, she fell again, face-first down the steps. Her fall took her directly onto the unforgiving concrete garage floor. No matter how I tried, there was no getting her up on her feet. Two others from the congregation joined me in the effort. She still could not stand. EMTs were called, and a trip to the emergency room ensued.

During the hours in ICU, x-rays were taken, and thankfully no broken bones were revealed. She was released from the hospital that evening to come home. They gave her some prescriptions to ease her pain, relax muscles, and reduce swelling. We settled in for the night after a tiring day.

Later that evening, Liz began making statements about seeing things that were not present. It was assumed that her *visons* resulted from the strong pain medication she had been prescribed. The effects of the medication would surely wear off as she slept.

I bounded into the living room where I had left her sleeping with great expectations at five the next morning. Nonetheless, she was found to be a bit more confused than the night before. Quickly, it was determined that medication would be left out of the mix moving forward. Her system could not handle it.

As we waited, time did not reduce the *effects* of her treatment. A couple of hours later, she got up to use the necessary room. She navigated in there slowly but deliberately. Yet on the trip back to her living room chair, she fell again in the hallway. Along with the help of a couple of friends, we were eventually able to get her up and back to her chair.

Still, it was clear that something was amiss. She was weak and unable to get up. There was no walking on her own. EMTs were called again, and we returned to the hospital.

Once there, the staff began to go beyond x-rays to run a battery of blood tests. They revealed a problem not at all associated with medication. Instead, her system was being battered with two extensive infections. She was in kidney failure and unable to fend off the sepsis. Her blood chemicals were seriously out of line. Her condition was grave. The waves of turbulence had increased in their veracity. Storm gale forces and the spray of the deep drenched us.

Everything the medical staff deemed necessary to bring stability was enacted. Yet their experience and strain in the face of the fury before bore little correction to the course. In the moment, I could place myself in the little fishing vessel with Jesus's disciples who were bombarded with the ferocity of a literal intense storm on the Galilean Sea. Mark records, "*But soon a terrible storm arose. High waves began to break into the boat until it was nearly full of water and about to sink*" (Mark 4:37 TLB).

These were seasoned fishermen. They had logged a lifetime of hours on the water. They knew its hazards and were well versed in how to address them. One can imagine that these veteran sailors exercised every intervention at their disposal—manipulating the sails, steering the rudder, driving the oars, and manning the buckets. Yet the moment was about to swamp them.

Then in the summit of their desperation, they remembered Jesus had been in the boat with them the entire voyage. In terror, they called out to Him. Again, Mark explained,

> The disciples woke him up, shouting, "Teacher, don't you care that we're going to drown?" When Jesus woke up, he rebuked the wind and said to the waves, "Silence! Be still!" Suddenly the wind stopped, and there was a great calm. Then he asked them, "Why are you afraid? Do you still have no faith?" (Mark 4:38–40 NLT).

Our boat and our storm were no different. The same question resonated from my lips. No doubt it did from Jesus as well.

As Tuesday began, I had hopes that the course to align her system would begin to address what was troubling her. It was her birthday, and my desires were high. Unfortunately, the contrary was true. Her condition worsened. Now beyond confusion, my brilliant bride could do little more than babble. The staff scheduled a dialysis treatment in hopes of helping her clear the impurities in her bloodstream. It was followed the next day with a second.

I sat next to her and held her hand while the second one was ongoing. The staff told me she was less than cooperative with the first. That kept it from being as thorough as it might have been. Me being with her seemed to keep her calm during the second treatment.

Nonetheless, as the dialysis was progressing well, a complication arose. Her heart rate accelerated—to very high levels. The team responded in a flash. I was ushered out of the room and down the hallway. The cart was brought into her room. Paddles had to be used on her heart to reset it. A million thoughts raced to my mind and one prayer—*Oh, God, I'm not ready to be without her.*

The treatment had been, thankfully, successful. Yet just as the waves of this episode had calmed, visiting hours ended. I had to leave. It was not what I wanted for sure. As you might imagine, I wanted to be with her. My daughters arrived from Michigan and would also like to see her. Yet COVID restrictions mandated that only one person per day can visit. Under normal conditions, one of us would have been with her around the clock. Frustratingly, those desires were not allowed.

Displeased, I left for home. Nonetheless, the attending nurse and team leader called me a couple of hours after my departure with a mixed bag of news. Her blood tests showed slight signs of improvement. Still, due to other visible concerns, they had to put her on a ventilator. Furthermore, the staff reported that she would soon be taken for a brain scan. There was concern there may have been bleeding or stroke caused by the heart rate episode. They noted she had been unresponsive since.

Visiting hours did not begin again until 10:00 a.m. I had no idea what to expect when I arrived. I had been assured if anything serious arose in between times her nurse would call. Somehow, that assurance brought little solace.

Back at the hospital, the process lingered on. Little progress was noticeable. Her system had been overtaken by infection. We had no clue. It had been undetected until the hours in the intensive care. Her prognosis was in question. Even though they have not been expressing the full force of the gravity she was facing, enough has been said to imply that rocky waters still faced us.

The hours ticked away. I was powerless to change the course before us. Still, as I whispered the burden of my heart to the throne of grace, I was assured that God heard every utterance. As He explained to the Old Testament prophet Jeremiah, "*Then you will call to me. You will come and pray to me, and I will answer you*" (Jeremiah 29:12 GNT).

I was confident He understood the breaking of my heart. Furthermore, I knew that the same One who raised Lazarus from the grave, when all thought it was beyond possibility, could raise up my wife from this grave condition. So I called out, waited, and rested in what only He could do.

During these unnerving hours of waiting, Liz rarely did more than mutter. Yet all of a sudden, something changed—if only for a moment. In one of her more lucid instants on Tuesday, I heard my wife also speaking—not to me, not to the medical team, but to the Lord. It was not babbling but purely conversational. Her words were spoken quietly but with intention—as if no one else was there. She quietly called out to Him for His touch, knowing He heard and could help.

Great confidence bolsters the believer along the tempestuous journey because the Master of the Sea is in the boat too. He listens as we express our fear. At His command, the waves grow smooth and the thundering winds still. Yet knowing the Master of the wind and the waves is sailing confidently with us stills the heart even as the tumult rages.

Even though the storm can be unnerving, my peace is not founded upon the fierceness of the gale that rages. I will wait confidently in Him.

CHAPTER 2

The Manifest Matters

Those who were inspired to chronicle the encounter with Jesus are a bit scant on the details of the fateful night of the storm that looked to swamp that fishing vessel. I'm thinking that one of my inquiries in eternity (there will no doubt be many) is to look up one of the disciples who were on the boat. I'd like to hear the story with all of the firsthand details. I'd like to look into their eyes as they recount those pulse-pounding moments as they combated the force of the storm. I'd like to hear how it was that they were able to overlook the reality of Jesus being with them all along. I'd enjoy listening as they floundered in faithlessness at that moment even though they had already witnessed Jesus do so many miraculous things.

I guess that my interest is piqued because I can relate. I can identify with turning to Jesus when I was out of options, when many avenues were pursued, yet there were no answers. Maybe it just reveals our very human side. The miracle worker is still able, is still sailing with His followers, and is still in the storm stilling business. Ultimately, it was the voice of the Master who overcame the source of the disciples' dread.

However, think back to the account of the Sea of Galilee gale-force encounter. Consider who was on board (besides Jesus!) during that fate-filled voyage. If I was to have set sail across that body of water two thousand years ago, I can think of none better equipped for the jaunt to the distant shoreline. The crew manifest matters.

While still young men, they were well-seasoned fishermen. They had amassed nearly a lifetime of hours on the water. As soon as they were old enough, they learned the craft hands-on from their fathers. Day in and day out, they took part in the family business. Navigating rough waves became secondhand. Storms were a constant factor in their line of work. They knew what to do.

In my imagination, I can picture them working together in harmony. No wasted motion. Everyone had a responsibility, and as the storm began to emerge, they jumped into action.

JOHN. Hey, fellows. Look off the port side. See that monster cloud rolling in over Mt. Hermon? We better get across to shore in short order.

PETER. [taking the vantage point on the bow] Andrew, man the sails. James, you take the rudder. The rest of you, pick up an oar. We have to—

JOHN. [cutting him off] That thing is moving in fast. And it is no short squall. It is massive. This is serious, guys. Find the nearest point to land and pick up the pace.

At that moment, the tempest hammered the little vessel. The waves crested above its sides. Each man was working tirelessly at their station—rowing, steering, and taking a drenching from the cloudbursts, the waves crashing over the sides, and spray from both pushed sideways by the near cyclonic winds. The vessel was taking on water and sinking under its weight.

In a moment, Peter shifted part of the rowing crew to man buckets and bail. Every member worked seamlessly with the others to see them through this unexpected storm. They were in these rough waters together.

That is the picture that comes to mind for me as our family encountered the vicious uncertainty of the dark clouds of these past hours. While I know that Jesus has been in the boat with us, there was an additional consolation. It came from a great outpouring of love from family and friends, as well as a faith family standing with us through this ordeal.

Our faith family has been praying with sincerity for my wife's healing and our resiliency. They stepped up to oversee my ministry responsibilities as I stayed as close to Liz at the hospital as possible. There were people who kept the prayer chain active and updated. While our congregation is on the smaller side, I felt the assurance of warrior legions at my side in this struggle. Seamlessly, they pulled together, stepping up to do what was possible to help us navigate through rough waters.

The impact of the love expressed was expansive. I have heard people say, "I don't need the church." That has not been my experience. I am so thankful for them—not just in this storm but also as we have encountered the pounding rains of turbulent circumstances over and again.

As I have heard it said, "There is nothing like the local church when the local church is working right." Until you find yourself on this side of difficulty, you cannot know how such support buoys the heart. There is something powerful about being part of a faith family that is *being* the church as demonstrated in the New Testament. With our greatest appreciation, our family is beyond grateful for ours. Their continued love, prayers, and authentic concern have been an unbelievable encouragement.

A crew willing to row, steer, sail, and bail together when storms arise (with Jesus in the boat!) is a recipe for a successful voyage. The manifest matters.

CHAPTER 3

The Twist of the Weather Vane

I am a big fan of classic family films. One which has stood the test of time and many generations is the great account of a once-in-a-lifetime nanny. She could look proudly into a mirror and confidently declare, "Practically perfect in every way." Mary Poppins's short stint with the Banks family consisted of memorable life-impacting adventures which not only altered the behavior of her two charges but, in the end, also metamorphosized an entire family and beyond.

Her influence on this family was so consequential that both her arrival and departure were marked by a change of the winds in their community. A large weather vane shifts to mark the turning force of the breeze. Bert, played by Dick Van Dyke, notices the changing surge and begins singing, "Winds in the east / There's a mist comin' in. Like somethin' is brewin' / And 'bout to begin. Can't put me finger on what lies in store. But I feel / What's to 'appen / All 'appened before." How quickly the weather changes and the twists of the lives on screen with it.

Yet, isn't that a picture of life? You're just sailing along. Life is uneventful, even tedious. The alarm rings at the same time as the day before. The routine is to ready for the next day on the job, tending to the affairs of the household, readying the kids for school, answering e-mails, and checking the to-do list one more time before heading out the door. Nothing has really prepared you for the turn of the storm front coming in your direction. It is just another day at the bank, in the car pool, or catching up with chores too long set on the back burner. As Paul McCartney once balladed, "It's just another day."

Then in an instant, out of the blue, lightning explodes across the sky. In a heartbeat, the winds shift, the weather vane twists, and the excursion of life jolts you into a far different place than you expected when the alarm bell sounded this morning.

The schedule of the adventure you are on has been blown off course. The winds wailed. The torrential rains descended. Another driver blows through a stop light and into your path. The doctor's office calls, saying, "The doctor needs to see you." A notice in the mail expresses that your identity has been stolen—along with life savings. Your teenage daughter says, "Mom, we need to talk." The weather vane twirls as the potent winds of change slam down from peaceful skies.

As Jesus slept in the boat and His disciples sailed across the lake toward the other side, a vicious storm blew in over the peaks of Mount Herman. Mark recorded, *"Suddenly a strong wind blew up, and the waves began to spill over into the boat, so that it was about to fill with water"* (Mark 4:37 GNT). Did you notice Mark's opening description? Suddenly. It was unexpected—even under the careful watch of seasoned men of the sea.

Such are the storm fronts that sweep down on placid lives. They had been undetected even under the scrutiny of watchful eyes. The barometric pressure swing had gone unobserved. The storm alarms hadn't sounded while the force of the gale and pounding cloudbursts slammed you. Your progress came to a halt.

Such sudden and violent storms are not uncommon in the region. These fishermen were well aware of their potential. They were also mindful of the overwhelming threat of such a surge. In the original language of the text, the disciples recognized that this was no shower that would quickly blow through and be done. There was a sense that its impact would be long, harsh, and devastating. Questions of survival shook their confidence. As they woke up Jesus, their concern is unmistakable in their question, *"The disciples woke him up and said, 'Teacher, don't you care that we are about to die?'"* (Mark 4:38 GNT).

Have you ever been there? Tranquil moments have been upended by the direct wallop of a torrent. Docile waterways were churned to menacing whitecaps that begin to lower you into the deep. Rowing and bailing appear to be fruitless. The daily routine has been thrown out to focus every bit of energy on keeping the vessel afloat.

I sat there in the stillness of Liz's hospital room. There was a constant array of chirps from devices and meters recording vitals. There were hoses and tubes connected from stem to stern pumping fluids in and taking them out. Yet little break from the tide that was battering my wife's health could be observed. The chill from the deluge encompassed the room.

When I got up early for my regular routine at church last Sunday morning, this scene had never crossed my mind. I was about to bring words of encouragement to my congregation. I would lead them in faithful prayer. Together, we would celebrate God's love and presence. There would be times to explore the message of God recorded in the scriptures. That is who I am. I am there to help others who find their situations challenging. It was just another day.

No change in the winds had been detected. Nevertheless, in a matter of moments, the weather vane had twisted. The raging swing in settings had been swift, unexpected, and overwhelming.

My wife lay still on her ICU bed. Her condition was not improving, and no break in the unrelenting tempest was in view. The mist of the rising tides was dampening my confidence. All I knew to do was sail, bail, and row. This storm was far more than my skill set could navigate.

Yet in the face of a storm-tossed voyage, I was reminded that it *was* just another day. Even though my situation had changed, Jesus had not. He was still in the boat and still adept. The storms did not raise His concern. He who created the wind was fully capable to manage it. The certainty that the Master of the Wind could bring calm with just a word, by faith, would quiet the tempest in my heart.

I have no idea what tomorrow will bring. Yet I'm trusting it and Liz to Him. There is a song by the Collingsworth Family that lifts my heart. The lyrics resonate with the truth of the Lord's faithfulness. It is entitled "Fear Not Tomorrow." Its message can bring encouragement in any stormy season:

> Are you troubled o'er things to come?
> Is your future unsure?
> And are you dreading the coming dawn?
> A long day to endure?
> Fear not tomorrow. God is already there.
> He's charting the course you take.
> He sees each hidden snare. He's waiting to guide
> you through each burden and care.
> Fear not tomorrow. God is already there.

Has a change in the winds brought you directly into the path of a storm? You have someone in the boat with you capable of what is coming your way. As Peter declared, *"So, humble yourselves under God's strong hand, and in his own good time he will lift you up. You can throw the whole weight of your anxieties upon him, for you are his personal concern"* (1 Peter 5:6–7 J.B. Phillips New Testament).

CHAPTER 4

When Day Breaks

There is something about daylight breaking over the murkiness of a long night that lifts the soul. It is a sense of new, of a clean slate, a renewed hope. The psalmist described the power of the dawn when life is experiencing the ebony of night.

Recorded in the thirtieth Psalm, the author, believed to have been David, expressed the light of hope restored by the unmistakable intervention of God. He exclaimed,

> I will praise you, Lord, because you rescued me... Lord, my God, I prayed to you, and you healed me... Sing praises to the Lord, you who belong to him; praise his holy name... Crying may last for a night, but joy comes in the morning... You changed my sorrow into dancing. You took away my clothes of sadness, and clothed me in happiness. I will sing to you and not be silent. Lord, my God, I will praise you forever. (Psalm 30 NCV)

Over the past week, our family experienced the falling of night. My wife, Liz, had become gravely ill. She has been an enigma for the hospital staff. Her body was overtaken by bacteria. Her kidneys began to fail. Her heart and blood pressure at times were erratic. For most of the week, she was unable to communicate, and what was spoken was little more than gibberish.

Like David, I prayed. Many who knew us did as well. In the night hours, many tears were shed. Pleas were extended. Our family was vigilantly before the Lord. Our faith family stood with us as well as pastors, churches, and staff at our movement's national office. People of faith all across the country were lifting us up to God. The notes of encouragement, commitments to seek God for our situation, and outpouring of love were so heartening.

As James commented in his New Testament letter, "*The earnest prayer of a righteous man has great power and wonderful results*" (James 5:16 TLB). The evidence of God's people praying was undeniable. I could feel the nearness of God even in the darkest moments. Later in the week, Liz's grave condition began to respond to the medication and treatment.

Daybreak has crested the horizon on the shadowy path walked by our family this week. Joy has awakened. Liz has taken substantial steps in her recovery—although we have been assured that her road back to health will be a lengthy one—several weeks or more. The hospital staff has removed many of the medical lines once attached to her. She is awake and was even making an occasional joke with our daughter this afternoon.

That progress did not mean daylight had burst on the scene. Just the glimmer of light that peeked through the darkness of the night sky was visible. Prayers were still needed. There was still much uncertainty awaiting the days before Liz and me. Many challenging steps were yet to be taken.

I had desired prayers not only for us but also for our congregation. They had been enduring a demanding season with the COVID-19 issues. While it had caused us to be creative in offering spiritual opportunities for our people, it has also caused immense stress on our ministries. Now add to it their pastor has been having his attention and energies a bit divided! All of these factors have the potential to stymie the kingdom's progress. I love my wife and cherish the work to which I have been called. I have been praying that through it all our united efforts grow stronger.

Rather than carrying a weight of concern, I then began to look forward to my arrival at the hospital each morning. God's *intervention took away my clothes of sadness, and clothed me in happiness.* Like David, I can proclaim, *I will sing to you and not be silent. Lord, my God, I will praise you forever.* Care to join me in a song of jubilation and thanksgiving?

Paul wrote to the believers of his generation, "*Always be full of joy. Never stop praying. Whatever happens, always be thankful. This is how God wants you to live in Christ Jesus*" (1 Thessalonians 5:16–18 ERV).

CHAPTER 5

The Trek Back

Today was day nine of our family's ordeal. Throughout the day, I was reminded of some certainties about healing and moving toward wholeness. The hospital medical staff has been forthright to me regarding Liz's trek to health. The acute infection of her system has drained her already-weakened condition. That state was led by a fall on the basement stairs about six weeks ago.

Her initial fall had damaged soft tissue in her hip, back, and leg. Her walking was hampered, eventually with a cane. She had been sleeping exclusively in the living room recliner. Climbing into bed was not going to happen. Additionally, as I jokingly told folks, I had become her chauffeur and was responsible for "driving Ms. Daisy."

Her condition was not improving. A follow-up visit to the doctor about two weeks before her hospitalization resulted in two appointments with physical therapy. Little could we foresee the train wreck that was on course in her system.

Without a medical intervention (and a divine one), I honestly believe she may not have overcome the poison within. The physicians have taken aggressive steps to break the cycle that was ravaging her life. A constant flow of medications, dialysis, and a host of other treatments addressed the condition that she could not overcome on her own.

On the mend from the infection that had gripped her, she moved from intensive care to a regular room and the next phase of her care. As today began, she had labored through all of her physical setbacks along with eight days of not moving from a bed. The hospital physical therapy team made their first visit to her room with the intention of getting her to her feet and into a chair. It was an exertive and valiant effort. Liz really tried. She was able to almost stand before being overcome again with weakness.

Undeterred, the PT team settled her back in bed and told her that they would be back tomorrow. She was assured with each application and effort she would be more successful. As she built up, the struggle would be less exhaustive. It was but the first of many baby steps toward physical heath.

There have also been conversations with the hospital social staff. They are working to secure Liz a place in her next phase of this journey. Once she is released from the hospital, she will be directly admitted to a rehab facility. Her treatment will continue there for an additional two to three weeks before she can actually come home.

Moving toward health takes time. As much as one might like it, wholeness is not instantaneous. Furthermore, it requires effort, dedication, and even discomfort. Without it, regression rather than advancement can be expected.

In observation of my wife's ordeal, I was struck not only by the realities of the healing process but also by profoundly spiritual parallels. In moving toward spiritual health and wholeness, the same can be surveyed.

First off, one's spiritual healing requires an *intervention*. Humanity is being poisoned by rebellion from God—sin. It is a malady that devastates each one within. As David observed, *"But all have turned their backs on him; they are filthy with sin—corrupt and rotten through and through"* (Psalm 53:3 TLB). The cure for what ailed us was beyond our capabilities. As Paul declared,

> But when the kindness of God our Saviour
> and his love towards man appeared, he saved
> us—not by virtue of any moral achievements of
> ours, but by the cleansing power of a new birth
> and the moral renewal of the Holy Spirit, which

he gave us so generously through Jesus Christ our
Saviour. (Titus 3:5 Phi)

Even though Paul stated that when one becomes a new creation in Christ, he becomes new on the inside, the move toward wholeness has only begun. It takes time. It is not instantaneous. Rather, it is a *progression* moving ever closer to the goal of wholeness—Christlikeness. Paul explained, *"And as the Spirit of the Lord works within us, we become more and more like him"* (2 Corinthians 3:18 TLB).

Authentic progression is the product of allowing God to change the person of faith in *cooperation* with his "prescribed treatment." Romans 12:2 (NLT) explains, *"Let God transform you into a new person by changing the way you think."* He brings to light those things that need to be removed, be altered, or be adopted into one's habits to develop them as a Christ follower.

Frankly, this will require exertion on the part of the believer as well as cooperation. God reveals the pathway to spiritual vitality through times of teaching, reflection upon His word, and in relationships of accountability. Peter wrote to his generation, *"Desire God's pure word as newborn babies desire milk. Then you will grow in your salvation"* (1 Peter 2:2 GNT).

Finally, the road to spiritual health will necessitate *determination*. There will be setbacks, discouragement, testing, trouble, and struggle. Remember that the outcome will be worth every step and strain toward the goal of wellness.

One of Liz's doctors told me that I must be willing to push her. He knew how important it was to keep her laboring forward. It is easy to settle for less than optimum health. Yet to do so would leave life short of its best. So I have already told her that I would be encouraging her during this challenging process.

As people of faith, let us help one another stay determined. Join with the writer of Hebrews who declared, *"And let us consider how we may spur one another on toward love and good deeds"* (Hebrews 10:24 NIV).

So where do you find yourself on the trek to health? Do you stand in need of an intervention of the Savior who offers redemption, restoration, and the realization of optimum living? Are you in the process of progression? Do you find the character of Jesus becoming incrementally more noticeable in your life? Can it be said that you are openly in cooperation with the adjustments God wants to bring about in you? Are you fully determined to become wholly made over in Christ? The trek toward spiritual health is not easy but always rewarding!

CHAPTER 6

The Waiting Game

I have come to understand where my virtues rest and, well, where I'm glad the divine construction project continues. Over these past days, I have been reminded that patience is one of those major works in progress. I understand that patience is one of the obvious fruits of the Spirit in the life of the Christ follower, but I can tell you that the ripening of fruit on this tree still needs some more time in the sun.

Although she is becoming more herself with each day, Liz's hospitalization is reaping more questions than answers. Her kidneys are now functioning, and the antibiotics are working. Yet her case is a puzzlement.

For any man, a woman is naturally an enigma of sorts. They are wired differently and have system functions that we fellows just have to take as fact. Yet right now, I would cherish some clarity.

The doctors have yet to identify the source of the infection in her system. Following two days of working with physical therapy, she still lacks the strength to stand. While I am so relieved at the improvement she has made, I find myself being short in the waiting department. I am yearning for development, for signs of improvement, and for evidence of health.

This is reflective of the current season of my life. I have been granted the privilege of serving as pastor of a loving church family. Liz and I have been at LifePoint now for three years. I am convinced that we are making wise ministry decisions. I sense the passionate desire of our leadership for this congregation to become a center of life change in our community. We have seen improvement in many factors. Yet questions linger. What will it take for the purposes of God to be more greatly realized in our ministries? There remains a yearning for evidence of health in every one of our ministry systems.

I find myself seeking answers. I know that there are hosts of people in our community whose lives would be so much richer with Christ at the center. Our church ministries and individuals have to find ways to bridge the divide keeping them from giving Christ a chance. The commission entrusted to us has not changed. Abundant and eternal life is weighing in the balance.

I know that there are great people in our congregation whose Christian experience would be more rewarding by investing a little time each week for biblical teaching in a growth group environment. What will it require to motivate them to reassign time? How can I engage them—adults and young people alike—more fully in order to better prepare them as believers in a culture pushing against their faith? They recognize the statement of the psalmist, *"Your word is like a lamp that guides my steps, a light that shows the path I should take"* (Psalm 119:105 ERV). Still, somehow, improving the glow of the lantern is not a priority.

I know that I am not alone in this quest. I speak to other ministry leaders who are contending with many of the same quandaries in their places of service. We struggle with leading our charges to health. The questions badger our hearts and trouble our sleep. It is the subject of more prayerful moments than the congregation understands.

We diligently yearn to lead our church families to be fully devoted followers of Christ—growing disciples who are becoming like Christ and are passionate about the things closest to the heart of Christ. We explore the sources of intrusion resisting the desired outcome. We seek answers from the Great Physician that lead to transformed lives. We watch and wait in anticipation of a breakthrough.

In addressing the believers of his generation, Paul instructed, *"And let us not get tired of doing what is right, for after a while we will reap a harvest of blessing if we don't get discouraged and give up"* (Galatians 6:9 TLB). I will continue leading and encouraging our church family toward spiritual health. When our systems are aligned with the Lord's, mountains are moved.

Tomorrow morning, I will be back at the hospital at ten when visiting hours begin. I continue to pray that God will give the staff the insight to discover Liz's health issues so they can be addressed. I will rely on the Great Physician to do what only He can do.

And I'll wait. I can't guarantee it will be patiently. Yet ultimately like the old song of the church expressed, "Many things about tomorrow, I don't seem to understand. But I know who holds tomorrow and I know He holds my hand."

CHAPTER 7

The Toughest Step to Take

There is an ancient proverb that observed, "The first step is always the hardest." I have seen that play out in our journey through Liz's health struggle. The drain of her system by the bacteria, which had overtaken it, had left her unable to lift herself, let alone stand.

A couple of days ago, the physical therapy team had tried unsuccessfully to help her to her feet. Once again yesterday, their efforts were fruitless. The infection remaining in her system is gathered around her hip. It has rendered her sapped of vitality. It is an issue concerning her medical attendants and physicians.

As I walked into her room this morning, I was immediately troubled. I could tell something was amiss. Her color was washed out. She was strikingly upset. I immediately began to question her about what had gone wrong. It wasn't *if* something had happened, but *what* it was.

Apparently, earlier in the morning, the heart episode she had experienced in the intensive care had reared its head again. This time, she felt it coming on. Her heart rate began to spike. She felt it "flutter" (to use her word). Clearly, what she had encountered had rendered her already-weakened state even more so.

The doctor had addressed the heart issue with an additional dose of medicine. He didn't act all that concerned about it. That is easy when it is not your system conducting a rapid-fire drum solo (please excuse my sarcasm).

Several times I have been told by attending staff how important it is to get her on her feet. Already twice she had fallen short of that goal—even with an honest effort. Now on day twelve of this journey, when she needed to find success in standing, her heart decides to get all excited and rob her of her already-depleted energy.

I stayed by her bedside through the day. As time ticked on, Liz's color returned. We chatted softly as often as she wanted. On and off she rested. Worship music continued to play in the background through the Bluetooth speaker I brought in several days before.

As the middle of the afternoon rolled around, strangely, the physical therapy team hadn't stopped in. I began to wonder if their appointment in Liz's room had been postponed due to the events earlier in the morning. As I told you yesterday, there was no guarantee that my waiting would be patient today. I began to talk to any of the attending staff who would listen. What was keeping the physical therapy staff from focusing on Liz's needs?

Just so that there will be no question, the hospital staff has been extraordinary. Even though stretched thin with all of the COVID-19 pressures, Liz has received exemplary care. These folks have a demanding job that keeps them hopping through the day. I have told them many times how much they are appreciated. Still, I pressed to make sure she would receive that needed visit today.

It wasn't but about ten minutes until they arrived. This time it happened. Two physical therapists and Liz's attending nurse worked to get her into position and assist her efforts. I could sense that Liz was really determined. It was the first step we had been praying to happen. She stood upright for the first time in twelve days—just about two whole minutes. Then after a short rest, they aided her to her feet again.

Soon, her exertion had expended her energy. The attending staff helped her back into bed. That initially determined stand was a milestone. It was the first step of what prayerfully will be many more as her healing process continues.

I want to thank the host of people who were praying for my bride and me. Words can never adequately express how much your partnership in our journey has meant to us. Please continue. This was just the first step—a difficult one to take to be sure—but just the first.

There may well be other "first steps" that should be the subject of your moments of intercession. How many people in your circles of influence need to take a step of faith to embrace Jesus as the forgiver of their past and to become the leader of their lives? That can be an enormously difficult step to take even though it will lead to a life filled with God's best. I know that there is someone in my circles that I pray for each day at 1:00 p.m. to take a step.

There are people you know who are in difficult circumstances. They feel trapped and unable to move past what is driving their unhealthiness. Pray that they will be determined enough to trust God and take that difficult first step toward a life that is purposeful and rewarding.

Maybe there is a step that you need to take. It is the moment of decision. Will you move past what has bound you in an unhealthy condition? You will find that if you are willing to brave that first step, God will meet you there. As was written, "*And when you draw close to God, God will draw close to you*" (James 4:8 TLB).

CHAPTER 8

The Moments Worth Treasuring

It was the aromas of a turkey roasting, bread baking, and all of the unbelievable trimmings along with the atmosphere of laughter that surged in my memories. Thanksgiving gathering at Grandma Cybil's was a highlight of the year. It was a chance to reconnect with a houseful of cousins, hear stories being retold, and take a respite from the turbulence that often resonated at home.

The setting was somewhat magical for a boy of nine. It left an indelible imprint in my mind. This was a season long before any of the families had "made it" financially. All were working-class laborers—police officers, GM workers, and office staff—trying to establish a more comfortable life. Yet, family holiday get-togethers which included each cousin's birthday were important events. It would take something fairly crucial to keep ones from attending. Something that may seem so small in today's generation was truly not small at all.

Memories were made. It was long before the tech generation which has infiltrated our culture. There is something so vital to human interaction that can never be replaced by a cell phone screen. What kind of memories will this generation have in reflective moments of adulthood? I, for one, will make a point of keeping my phone in my pocket so my attention can be given to the people whose relationships with me matter most.

We are beginning week three of Liz's hospital stay. I know there are many of you who have walked that sort of journey for a much longer period. I'm not sure about your experience, but I have had many moments to consider and reset priorities during this trek. I have come to examine those things so frequently taken for granted and realize the gravity of their importance. I have been brought to renewed gratitude for little things.

As I walked into Liz's room yesterday after church, I was met with a blessed surprise. She was not, as I had become accustomed to for the past two weeks, just resting in bed. Rather, physical therapy had been in and had her up walking a few steps, and she was now sitting in a chair eating her lunch. For the next four hours, she was able to sit in the chair, peer out the window, and take in the sunshine. It was therapeutic for both of us (even though it meant me sitting on the floor part of the time)!

On the outside, some might think this is really not a big deal. I suppose it depends on the perspective of the one on the journey. Less than two weeks before, I wasn't sure that I would be bringing her home. I didn't know if our journey together might be cut short. Every moment, every incremental improvement, every step forward may seem small. Yet during this Thanksgiving season, I have been reminded how significant it is to be thankful for the little things.

A passage from Colossians has settled in with renewed authority. As Paul wrote to the believers of his day, he beckoned them, "*Let the peace of heart that comes from Christ be always present in your hearts and lives, for this is your responsibility and privilege as members of his body. And always be thankful*" (Colossians 3:15 TLB).

I know that the journey ahead will yet be strenuous. Ms. Liz has some challenges before her. Yet I will be thankful for the miles we will yet walk together, the memories we will share, and the future God has waiting for us.

CHAPTER 9

Measure Twice

I'm not totally sure of its source. Maybe it is a convulsion of deficiencies. Heaven knows that I have my share. First off, I'm a guy. Guys tend to be fixers—assess, address, and progress. In addition, anyone who knows me understands my ADD tendencies. Whatever the case, it can lead to overly rapid estimation of situations that arise.

Now that we have hopefully moved past the most acute moments of Liz's recent health complications, I find many moments in the stillness of her hospital room to reflect. This bombardment of infection in her body has really taken a toll on her energy. Her moments with physical therapy along with not getting extensive sleep time (I mean who really is allowed to sleep in the hospital?) really drains her. While my dear bride wants me there with her during visiting hours, there is ample time when she settles in for well-needed rest. It is time that has caused me to be quiet and ponder things as well.

There are natural things like realizing how fragile life can be and how crucial it is to not take moments for granted. There are reminders of just how blessed I have been for these nearly forty-three years. I have known love, companionship, support, encouragement, and, as needed, gentle reminders of my shortfalls. I know what it means to look into her eyes and know what it means for two to become one.

A new area of reinforcement has struck me in the quiet times over these past few days. As the pieces of Liz's health puzzle have been put into place, I realized that I need to really be careful about making snap assessments. As I have reviewed in my mind these past weeks, I was struck by how many times I was too quick to judge.

The medical team feels that Liz's current health situation arose about seven weeks ago. She fell coming up the basement stairs and landed fairly firmly on her hip and leg. When she told me what she had done, I chuckled, shook my head, and didn't think much about it. She would be sore and nicked up for a few days. It's not like this is the first time my wife's propensity for mishap has arisen.

In the weeks that followed, she was not improving. She slowed down and became more lethargic, spending most of her hours at home in the recliner with a heating pad. Walking became more labored. I thought she should just work it out, stretch, and walk. She was just not trying hard enough—at least in my mind. The doctor found nothing broken. It didn't occur to me that there was something internal that was degrading. It was just a combination of getting older, arthritis, and a lack of motivation. Again, my assessment lacked insight into her reality. I was wrong. A really tough acknowledgment.

On Sunday morning of her first ambulance ride, I had come home to pick her up and drive her to church. I checked on her and went to the car to make sure it was warm. I saw her come out the door into the garage. When I looked up again, the door was closed, but Liz was nowhere to be seen. I waited, assuming she had forgotten something, and went back inside.

The wait became a few minutes. A bit upset at the delay, I got out of the car to go back inside. I would find out what was taking her so long and, if I could, assist her progress. As I walked around the side of the other car parked in the garage, I spotted her laying down on the garage floor. She had fallen and was unable to get herself up. Again, snap judgment, errant evaluation.

I brought her back from the hospital that night. X-rays proved negative, and she felt she could manage. She was prescribed a pain killer, anti-inflammatory, and muscle relaxer. She took her first dose and took her place in her easy chair. Just a few hours later, she began having mild hallucinations. Patterns were showing on a white wall. I attributed it to the effects of the pain killer, chuckled, and believed it would wear off by morning.

I arose about 5:00 a.m. She was awake in her chair. My normally very together wife's reality was very confused. I chalked it up to her possibly taking another dose of the medication while I was asleep. Again, uninformed rapid assessment missed the mark. If only I had listened to the advice of my friend the carpenter, measure twice, cut once.

Shortly after, she had yet another fall. This time in the hallway. The EMTs were called again. In the emergency treatment room, her confusion continued. It was not the medication but the infection running roughshod over her body. Soon her kidneys shut down—the opening credits to the drama that has played out for the past seventeen days.

One has to be careful making a hasty determination of someone else's situation. I'm sure I'll have to strive more carefully even now. Consider the example of Jesus. He called Matthew from the tax collector's booth to follow Him. The Romans hated Matthew because he was a Jew. The Jews hated him because he worked for the Romans. The religious leaders saw Matthew and his fellow tax collectors as scum. Jesus saw him as a life that had been misdirected by greed and invited him to be a part of His inner circle. Following Jesus would reset the trajectory of his life.

Jesus was once having dinner at the house of Simon the Pharisee. A woman came into the banquet room. She stood behind him, weeping. Luke describes it this way,

> As they sat down to eat, a woman of the streets—a prostitute—heard he was there and brought an exquisite flask filled with expensive perfume. Going in, she knelt behind him at his feet, weeping, with her tears falling down upon his feet; and she wiped them off with her hair and kissed them and poured the perfume on them. (Luke 7:36–38 TLB)

The Pharisee looked at her with scorn. She was "that kind of woman." She looked at Jesus in remorse. She had a story of which the Pharisee knew nothing. Jesus saw her through the eyes of grace and redemption. She left that day with a fresh start.

May we guard ourselves against quick judgment. Take time to listen. Open up to love.

CHAPTER 10

Lessons from the A-Team

"Hannibal" Smith was the leader of the great television program *The A-Team*. It was broadcast during the 1980s. Hannibal was known for a saying that normally surfaced after nearly an hour of chaos on the program. He would sit back smiling smugly and declare, "I love it when a plan comes together."

Yet don't we all have a little of Hannibal in us? We chart a course, determine the desired outcome, and celebrate its achievement. Nevertheless, can I see the hands of those whose plans did not end up the way they had them charted in their minds? How about those who arrived at their desired destination only to discover it looked nothing like what was depicted on the brochure?

The trek we have been on with Liz's heath crisis for the past nearly three weeks falls under that category. With the physical therapy she's been undergoing at the hospital, the bombardment of antibiotics, and rest, her improvement has been really encouraging. The plan in all of this effort was to get her well enough to leave the hospital and begin extended rehabilitation.

This afternoon, we were given the news. A place had opened up at the rehab facility we had been targeting. In my pastoral experience with other patients there, I was highly impressed by the staff and their level of care. She was to be moved tonight.

It was a bit surprising, however. I was told that the facility would contact me by phone for details if and when a spot opened.

No call had come. We were given the news by the nursing staff at the hospital. They would transport Liz by ambulance following visiting hours at the hospital.

As the time for her transfer came, I was given a bit of further insight that had not been in any way anticipated. The rehab facility is literally right next door to the hospital. We could look out Liz's room window and see it clearly. It belongs to the same health system as the hospital. I felt it reasonable that the same visiting privileges would be followed.

During Liz's ordeal, I had been with her, tending her, and helping to make her stay more comfortable from ten in the morning until six at night. She wanted me there even as she was napping. The quiet times afforded me time to read and write as well as put her at ease.

However, the county manager put further squeezes on the mobility of the populace in his effort to get a handle on the COVID-19 spike in the county. Personally, I believe this approach does more unintended harm than it does good. It adds unwarranted stress to families and unnecessary economic hardship to businesses, with little concrete evidence of reducing the mobility of the virus. But this is not a place for me to rant.

Liz will begin at least two weeks of concentrated rehabilitation in the morning. If that proves true, she will be home and able to enjoy a little Christmas celebration in the familiar surroundings of her own place. She is in the facility we had hoped that she would be, getting the kind of care we longed for her to receive. Yet in the meanwhile, due to the county lockdown, I will be forbidden from seeing her, encouraging her progress in person, and reinforcing how much she is loved. For at least two weeks! I love it when a plan comes together—it so rarely happens.

While I am uncomfortable with the arrangements, it is just another leg of this journey. As I have rested this ordeal in God's capable hands up to now, I will trust His wisdom for what is yet upon us. The destination was not exactly as was pictured on the brochure. Some of the amenities I looked to enjoy were not a part of the package. Solomon once observed, "*Many are the plans in a person's heart, but it is the Lord's purpose that prevails*" (Proverbs 19:21 NIV).

I'm not sure what God is bringing about to advance His purpose through this time of difficulty in our lives. Still, I want to fulfill His intentions even if they sideline my plans in the duration. One day, I'm certain that we will become more aware of how this time of discomfort advanced his objectives. As Paul declared to the believers of his generation, *"And we KNOW that in ALL things God works for the good of those who love him, who have been called according to his purpose"* (Romans 8:28 NIV, emphasis mine).

It is my prayer that the time of this next stop along our journey passes quickly, Liz's restoration is complete, and God's objectives are furthered. May His kingdom be advanced in our lives and furthered through them.

CHAPTER 11

Thunder in a Whisper

What is it about people that causes them to expect God to show up in their lives and to reveal Himself in stunning ways? Why do we expect some great signs? After all of the remarkable miracles (unexplained supernatural interventions of God) demonstrated out in the open for the multitudes to experience, the calls for greater proof continued to be demanded.

Mark recorded one of those occasions in the life of Jesus. "*Now the Pharisees came out and began an argument with him, wanting a sign from Heaven. Jesus gave a deep sigh, and then said, 'What makes this generation want a sign?*" (Mark 11:12 Phi).

I have been guilty of this myself. I know that the same God who whispered and the cosmos were flung into the regions of space could show Himself in a manner that would leave us bewildered. I have prayed some pretty audacious prayers. They were requests asking for God to reveal Himself in ways that no one could question His hand was involved.

I can attest there have been moments when the intervention of God has been powerful and undeniable. Nonetheless, far more often in my experiences, I have found God showing up in subtle, unexpected ways. Today has been one of those days.

Now don't jump to conclusions. It's not that my moments were filled with sunshine, roses, and bubble gum. Quite the contrary. Due to the restrictions of our county with spikes in COVID-19 cases, our church was meeting virtually only. The Sunday proclamation of the message was done before an iPad and one person at the tech desk. As I told someone yesterday, it would be a bit easier if there were at least cardboard cutouts of the congregation in the chairs!

Don't get me wrong. I am truly thankful for the technology to communicate in this manner. God's word is going out, and as God assures,

> The rain and snow come down from the heavens and stay on the ground to water the earth. They cause the grain to grow, producing seed for the farmer and bread for the hungry. It is the same with my word. I send it out, and it always produces fruit. It will accomplish all I want it to, and it will prosper everywhere I send it. (Isaiah 55:10–11 NLT)

I trust that God will do so with the message broadcast. Still, for me, virtual church lacks the sweet interpersonal connection with the church family. Add to it, my love, partner, and dearest friend rests ten miles away in a rehab hospital. Even though she is not well, I miss being with her. Furthermore, this was not a good day for her. The infection in her system is still trying to raise its ugly head. She is feverish and drained, and I'm kept from being there to care for her. It's disheartening.

I went over to the church early this morning to prepare the technology and take care of a few other items to ready the facility for today's broadcast. Worship music played quietly as I completed the arrangements for the morning. I sat down and just begin to pray. I have been wrestling with how to move ahead into the new year. There are so many unknowns with the pandemic and the limited resources of pastoring a smaller congregation—human resources, financial resources, and the like. While I am not twenty-nine years old any longer, I still tend to be pretty energic and am determined to allow my life to further God's purposes. Yet there are realities confronting the *want-tos*.

As I prayed, I just reiterated that God already knows my heart. How I want to know that we are making a difference. It is my yearning to see lives transformed by Christ to grow in their faith and be engaged as people of faith in expanding the kingdom of God. How I needed to hear from Him. I needed to see, dare I say it, a sign.

I'd like to say that God brought down fire from heaven, shook the earth, or a whirlwind of revival broke out. But as Elijah discovered, God wasn't necessarily in those things.

> And as Elijah stood there, the Lord passed by, and a mighty windstorm hit the mountain. It was such a terrible blast that the rocks were torn loose, but the Lord was not in the wind. After the wind there was an earthquake, but the Lord was not in the earthquake. And after the earthquake there was a fire, but the Lord was not in the fire. And after the fire there was the sound of a gentle whisper. When Elijah heard it, he wrapped his face in his cloak and went out and stood at the entrance of the cave. (1 Kings 19:11–13 NLT)

In the moments following my time of prayer, there was that whisper. Oh, not a physical one, but the still, small voice of God reminding me that He hears. I was checking on the recording device, and the door of the church opened. A gentleman walked in. He lives just blocks from the church. His family is looking for a place to connect. We discussed what was taking place and how due to COVID restrictions we are only broadcasting online for the next four weeks. He asked me to hold them up in prayer, looked me in the eye, and said they would be back.

As the newcomer departed, the floodgates opened, and I began to weep. There was no doubt of his presence—the Lord passed by. To paraphrase the song, "I raised a hallelujah!" God knew the assurance I needed at the moment.

Yet, He wasn't done. He took a second lap for good measure. Following the recording this morning, I went back home and waited for Liz to call. That is our arrangement—not knowing when she will be in therapy or resting. The day drug on and yet no call. She had requested a couple of things from home and for me to pick up some of her laundry. The exchange would be made by hospital staff while I waited in the lobby.

Her request was granted, and the staff attendant told me that she had been resting and would call me. I hadn't eaten so I drove to the next county to a favorite restaurant. While I was waiting on my meal, Liz called. Apparently, she had fallen back asleep again. It was during that conversation that she relayed that she was struggling with the infection. She was feverish and yet chilled all at the same time. I encouraged her to cut our conversation short and rest though I cherished every moment. There would be more time when she was well.

We hung up. My dinner arrived, and I ate quietly, thinking about all of the happenings of the day. As I finished, I called on the server to get my bill. She smiled and, in her heavy Asian accent, told me that someone in the restaurant had already paid it. They just wanted to be a blessing to me this Thanksgiving season. I was floored. Yep, He passed by again. He had thundered in a whisper.

If there was anything to be gained from today's experiences, it is this: Watch closely. God often shows up in ways that can be overlooked. Listen for the whisper of the Almighty. Being granted an audience with the miraculous is something special. Yet what can be grander than the whisper of the Heavenly Father spoken directly to you that declares, "I love you," "I hear you," and "I am with you"?

CHAPTER 12

With the Finish Line in View

Yesterday was an incredibly important day. For the past twenty-four days—the entire month to this point—our family has been in the midst of a grueling process. If you have been following the posts, you know that my precious bride has been in the hospital. It began with a weakening of her body, a series of falls, delirium, and then very disquieting days in intensive care. By the time she was able to be relocated into a regular room, Liz was so weakened she was unable to get out of bed for several days.

Under the great care of the hospital staff and the steady hand of God bringing her along, she finally was discharged from the main hospital. The move was not home, but to a rehabilitation hospital on the same medical campus. Her progress there has been arduous. Daily, the efforts to restore her mobility have become more demanding but have expanded her capabilities. Yet her road to recovery will require many further incremental steps.

Nevertheless, I was contacted by the rehabilitation team yesterday afternoon to explain that Liz is projected to be discharged in ten days. Finally, there is a tangible goal that has been established. We have been given a finish to this leg-of-her race. She will be able to again be in the welcome surroundings of home.

The team made it clear that there will be many more miles ahead once she arrives back in the homeplace. She has to remain on intravenous antibiotics for a few weeks following her release. Home health care visits will be initiated. Follow-up trips to various doctors who have cared for her during her hospitalization will be necessary. Continued physical therapy and exercise will be required to regain her mobility. And any of you who knows my wife knows she was already plotting her course back to work.

Yet, let's not get ahead of ourselves. I just want to bask in the long-awaited announcement that the finish line of these days of separation and struggle is nearing a conclusion. It is within view.

This announcement came about on a day when another finish line was crossed by someone dear to us. I received a call yesterday morning that Liz's uncle Norman had passed away. He had been fighting a valiant lengthy fight with pneumonia. While I had been praying for my wife, I had also been praying for him and his family who were unable to visit him at the hospital due to the pandemic.

Uncle Norm was a dear saint of God who loved his family and his church, loved to fish, and was deeply devoted to Jesus Christ. For Norm, the long days of separation and struggle came to an end, not just separation from family and struggle with illness, but from the very existence he had longed to claim much of his life. He had crossed the finish line.

While he loved life, there was always a greater reality in view. He served the Lord with gladness in this life but had his sight set on a distant shore. Like Paul, he too felt the pull from what awaited. Paul declared there is a "groaning" within for the homecoming.

Norm lived in faith of Jesus's proclamation,

> Don't let your hearts be troubled. Trust in God, and trust in me. There are many rooms in my Father's house; I would not tell you this if it were not true. I am going there to prepare a place for you. After I go and prepare a place for you, I will come back and take you to be with me so that you may be where I am. (John 14:1–3 NCV)

I was told that the hospital allowed Norm's wife and children to speak with him in the waning moments of his life. They were able to express their love for him. It was also relayed to me that his expression suggested he wanted to speak to them but wasn't able.

He was truly prepared for the moment that would soon come. I'm sure had he been able, he would have expressed his love for them all. He would have also assured them of his confidence for the hour that awaited.

Maybe like Paul to his protégé, Timothy Norm would have declared,

> The time for my departure is near. I have fought the good fight, I have finished the race, I have kept the faith. Now there is in store for me the crown of righteousness, which the Lord, the righteous Judge, will award to me on that day—and not only to me, but also to all who have longed for his appearing. (2 Timothy 4:6–8 NIV)

Uncle Norman finished his race. He kept the faith. No more separation. No more struggle. He is finally enjoying the welcome surroundings of home.

CHAPTER 13

Roads Under Construction

It has been a long time coming. Smooth roads. During the past three years that we have been in our North St. Louis County home, the road in front of the house has been in various stages of patchwork, holes, and crumbling asphalt. I have been amazed at the speed folks have traveled by in light of the conditions.

Still, over the past few months, a major undertaking has been initiated. The road has been stripped and is being resurfaced. All of the crumbling sidewalks have been removed and replaced with new concrete and reconfigured with handicap-accessible curbs. The final layer of asphalt will be set in the next few days. Smooth roads.

Yet there are problems with smooth roads. First off, what little restraint had been taken to navigate the way before and during construction has been cast aside. What is marked as a thirty-five miles per hour speed limit isn't often heeded as a suggestion. It is not uncommon to see cars fly by at what would be a considered reckless rate. Concerning is thinking about people backing out of their driveways or pulling out of side streets in light of travelers zipping by on accommodating pavement. A mishap was a possibility even before the road was smooth. Wisdom must accompany the journey.

Furthermore, the former pavement on our street in all of its disrepair had once been a smooth road. Conditions change, sometimes suddenly (take it from a guy who spent much of his life around Michigan potholes!). Time has its ways of altering the surface of the roads on which we travel. We enjoy smooth traveling yet find bumps along the way upsetting.

The statement is just as valid with the experiences of life. Our journey had a bit of that just yesterday. For the past five days, Elizabeth was progressing in her rehabilitation. The staff had been complimenting her efforts and improvement. She is on track to be released to come home in six days (yes, I have been counting them down!). Still, after five days of advancement, yesterday, she hit a pothole. One of her knees is throbbing with pain, and her medicine is giving little relief. Add to it, due to COVID restrictions, I cannot be with her to comfort her and encourage her.

I tried to remind her of the great progress she had been making. It had been five days since she had a setback. That was really encouraging, considering the slow laborious trek she'd been on for the past almost four weeks. She had come so far from where she had been. Her return home was just days away.

She acknowledged those observations. Yet they really didn't mute her displeasure with how she was feeling. She understood that her rehabilitation would not always be paved with smooth roads, but it didn't help that this portion of the way was still under construction. It was uncomfortable, unsettling, and unpleasant.

I was reminded that what she was experiencing really is a metaphor for the human experience. For some reason, people just expect nothing but smooth roads. When troubled miles come along our journey, they take us by surprise. We get angry, weepy, anxious, and even call God's love for us into question.

All the while, Jesus explained that bumps and potholes will accompany each of us on this side of eternity. With the shadow of the cross before Him and the reality that His disciples would all not stand with Him, Jesus told His disciples, *"I have told you all this so that you may find your peace in me. You will find trouble in the world— but, never lose heart, I have conquered the world!"* (John 16:33 Phi).

I suggest that you go back and read Jesus's statement again slowly. Deliberately. Was there any question that this life would be marked by challenges and hardships? You *will* find trouble in the world. Maybe better said, trouble will find you!

Following Christ's resurrection, each of these disciples became bold advocates for Jesus and leaders of the Christian movement. Still, their lives were marked by great hardship and even martyrdom. They were standing for all of the right things and doing what was expected, yet they were not spared rough roads.

The Apostle Paul was a steady champion for Jesus and His church. From his pen, a majority of the New Testament is credited. Nevertheless, he spent much of his ministry behind bars for his faith.

He noted,

> I have been in prison more often. I have suffered terrible beatings. Again and again I almost died. Five times the Jews gave me 39 strokes with a whip. Three times I was beaten with sticks. Once they tried to kill me by throwing stones at me. Three times I was shipwrecked. I spent a night and a day in the open sea. I have had to keep on the move. I have been in danger from rivers. I have been in danger from robbers. I have been in danger from my fellow Jews and in danger from Gentiles. I have been in danger in the city, in the country, and at sea. I have been in danger from people who pretended they were believers. I have worked very hard. Often I have gone without sleep. I have been hungry and thirsty. Often I have gone without food. I have been cold and naked. (2 Corinthians 11:23–27 NIRV)

Not many smooth roads there.

Return to the statement of Jesus to His disciples. "*I have told you all this so that you may find your peace in me…never lose heart, I have conquered the world!*" We have found great comfort in the undeniable presence of the Lord through this journey we have been on over this past month. Smooth roads? Not always. There have been some potholes. But when the turbulence comes (and it does), our peace is in the one who travels with us and has already claimed victory.

Anticipation

Anyone who has known me knows that I am a visual learner. Therefore, I connect with media. While there has been superb story-telling in motion pictures, I contend to you that the most innovative and creative moments are captured in the thirty–sixty-second spots used to advertise on television.

Consider the multimillions of dollars invested in airing ads on the Super Bowl broadcast each year. While the game may be memorable or mediocre, what people talk about at the water cooler the next day are the commercials. When one captures the imagination, it pays dividends in raising corporate visibility.

Not all memorable ads have been generated by Super Bowl coverage. They create an iconic identity with a product or service that continues on in the mind of their audience. For example, the phrase "Can you hear me now?" has left a mark on the discussion on cell phone reliability. Whenever you see a billboard featuring large cows discussing chicken, your mind is drawn to Chick-fil-A.

Another that I recall from several years ago has retained its place in my memory. The ad spot featured the great '70s song "Anticipation." While the song plays in the background, various faces watched with longing and eagerness for thick catsup to finally make its way out of the bottle onto their waiting plates.

There is something about a feeling of anticipation, the expectation of something good awaiting that motivates us. We shake and tap the catsup bottle in hopes of hurrying the process (even though we really appreciate catsup that is not runny!). We sit by the phone wanting no other distractions because of a call we've been told is coming. There is real power in anticipation.

I am captured by that sense of anticipation as I write. It has been projected that Elizabeth is scheduled to come home from what will be nearly five weeks in the hospital—in just three days! In anticipation of her homecoming, I am working extended hours to get a number of projects done around the house.

Some are making sure the house is handicap accessible for her. I am clearing any obstructions to her limited movement as she continues to rehabilitate. Others are striving to make sure that the environment is as perfect as I can make it. There is additional cleaning, rearranging, decorating, and wrapping Christmas presents (wrapping is not an acquired skill so I know that it must be a labor of love!). There have been additional trips out searching for the items she'll need once she gets home. I looked at my watch last night as it neared ten-thirty I was standing in line at the store.

The thrust of this anticipation has also yielded some unintentional projects. For example, I hurriedly loaded the washing machine while in the middle of doing some other things. One of the items needing washing was my jacket. The only problem was I forgot about putting a couple of disposable face masks in the pocket earlier in the evening. Do you have any idea how much paper sheds a face mask leaves all over your laundry? Neither did I. After two more washing and vacuuming out the washer and dryer several times, I did add a mental note to make sure I check pockets before washing.

While I was a bit flustered with myself, I really didn't let it get to me. Anticipation ruled the day. There was much to get ready. A few mishaps and mistakes would not change what was coming. I needed to stay on task and make sure I was getting things ready. Elizabeth would be coming. I so wanted her to be pleased with her arrival.

If only Christ followers would live in such anticipation that it would shape the way that they approach life. Since the time that Jesus returned to the side of the Heavenly Father, we have lived in the reality of His return. On that day Jesus's disciples watched Him rise into the heavens, they continued staring heavenward. They were convinced His return was imminent. Angelic messengers spoke to them to say, "*Galileans, why are you standing there looking up at the sky? This Jesus, who was taken from you into heaven, will come back in the same way that you saw him go to heaven*" (Acts 1:11 GNT).

Before His leaving, Jesus had given final instructions stating what they were to be doing in the meanwhile. For three years, He had explained the purposes for which they were living. He would be returning. Their marching orders were clear.

Nothing has changed other than the reality that we are two thousand years closer to Christ's return. Have our marching orders changed? Just how should we be living today in light of His return? Are we living in anticipation of it or as if there is nothing to concern us? As John penned to the believers of his generation,

> And now, children, stay with Christ. Live deeply in Christ. Then we'll be ready for him when he appears, ready to receive him with open arms, with no cause for red-faced guilt or lame excuses when he arrives. (1 John 2:28 MSG)

CHAPTER 15

On the Back Side of the Torrent

Our journey these past months has been anxious, arduous, and adventurous. That is the nature of storm-tossed middle-of-the-night sailing.

I can personally attest that there are impressionable moments in which you discover a great deal about yourself. You are reminded of the value of your faith. You are struck by the significance of being a part of a community of faith and a loving network of people who hold you up with encouragement and bring your situation up before the throne of grace.

While our trek along the lane toward Liz's full restoration is far from complete, there have been enormous strides along it. Her doctors have been revealing to her in recent visits how gravely ill she really was. They are speaking in terms that they did not in the height of her initial ordeal. They really weren't confident of her prognosis even with their treatment. There were elements of the storm that the professionals did not fully reveal. Yet God was fully aware.

I was shaken by the veracity of the storm that I was experiencing. The winds were howling with gale-force impact. The waves were towering. Yet, in the torrent, there was an unmistakable still small voice of the One in the vessel with me bringing calm to a very shaken soul.

The miles on the rough seas have been challenging. I've watched my dear bride struggle to regain her strength and independence.

Hours of rehabilitation have been a part of her experience. Her system has been bombarded with strong antibiotics, pain medication, and a sense of determination to make every stride necessary to regain all of her physical abilities.

She has shown great improvement. The torrential rain has subsided and is now just an annoying shower. The waves beneath us have settled to much more navigable levels. It may be that we are on the back side of the torrent.

Without the anxiousness of facing down the uncertainty of a dark of night hurricane, and with a bit of a break from the demands of ongoing attention to the storm, some time has been given to reflect. There has been much learned and affirmed during this season of struggle. On the back side of the torrent, it is an occasion to put things into perspective.

Reflecting upon the miles taken through this stormy season, I have come to see the unfathomable power of God. It is a strength that bolsters hope in the distressed and confidence in the unnerved. It is a potency that lets one rest in uncertainty. The statement of Paul to the believers of his generation took on a very personal application. *"Christ is the one who gives me the strength I need to do whatever I must do"* (Philippians 4:13 ERV).

It can be for certain that the storm through which we have passed will not be the last. Jesus said, *"You will find trouble in the world—but, never lose heart, I have conquered the world!"* (John 16:33 Phi). The power afforded me as a Christ follower gives me assurance that there is no squall beyond his capability in me.

God has been a faithful companion through this stormy excursion. He has been a capable ally. I have observed His hand at work, felt His obvious presence, and am in awe of his power. I have been reminded of the statement of his befuddled disciples in their stormy sea experience—*"Who is this man, that even the winds and seas obey him?"* (Mark 4:41 TLB).

One final reflection has settled on my mind on the back side of the torrent. In the case of Jesus and His disciples following their storm-tossed night at sea, they landed on shore and were met by a very different challenge. It also revealed an opportunity to make an impact in someone's life (Mark 5).

God has brought us through the challenges of the storm we've encountered, not just to sit in awe. The days ahead that we are given are an opportunity to encounter the lives of people who need to know the "storm chaser." He is the one who can meet them in the place of their storm and bring hope, healing, and restoration to their lives.

I can't say that bearing the brunt of the storm was enjoyable. Yet it was good to be reminded of how capable He is in the teeth of the storm. It was an inescapable reminder of how present He always is in the boat as we sail. Clarity was given to the way His power enables us through inevitable torrents life brings our way. That is a message people need to hear. He is the One they need to know. I have been given the privilege to share my story.

As John noted in his Gospel account,

> The disciples saw Jesus do many other miraculous signs in addition to the ones recorded in this book. But these are written so that you may continue to believe that Jesus is the Messiah, the Son of God, and that by believing in him you will have life by the power of his name. (John 20:30–31 NLT)

CHAPTER 16

Milestones

Have there ever been times when listening to a conversation you wonder if you have stepped into a different dimension? Or maybe another culture? A couple of years ago, our church upgraded its worship presentation software. The young couple who had been serving as a lead in the worship team moved out of state, and people were depending upon me to teach the staff working the new software how to navigate the upgrade.

Never shy about a challenge, I dove in. I mean, how hard can it be? I've done presentations before—different software, sure—so I can figure this out. Besides, this software comes with an extensive video tutorial—on-screen instructions for dummies.

After trying to navigate the software on my own for a bit, I found I could use a little insight into best practices. (In other words, I messed up long enough and finally gave in to following the instructions!) I clicked on the opening video tutorial with great anticipation. A smiling correspondent from the company was ready to serve.

Yet, shortly after he began, I knew this would not be as informative as I had hoped. He was a fast talker (or I was a slow listener), and he was using terminology that did not connect with this novice's vocabulary. Words took on a different meaning as if coded to an underground society.

I've noticed, especially in the past decade, that a number of words have been redefined by our culture—not always in a positive way but that is for a different discussion. However, in sizing up the journey upon which we set sail last November, another term has taken on a very different implication. It is the word *milestone*.

A milestone had been seen as something substantial, something for which humans marked their calendars. It was something that one could look back at and see the profound mark it had imprinted upon the progress of humanity. Milestones included such cultural shifts as the onset of the industrial revolution, the explosion of the information and technology industries, the end of the cold war, and the landing on the moon. Big happenings. Game changers.

Those sorts of happenings had been how my mind processed the definition of a *milestone*. That is until our boat set sail on this new course in our lives. When you are braving the storm of trial, small things become monumental. Small victories become ticker-tape parade celebrations. To others, they may seem trivial; but when navigating the rough seas toward the hope of the shoreline, the trivial is consequential.

In the anxiousness of the intensive care days when a spouse is faced with those words "*clear!*" knowing the outcome may not be positive, rest assured a steady and calmed heartbeat is a milestone. The move out of ICU to a *regular* room is as well.

In the tempest, the minute advances become enormous leaps. Removal of the ventilator. Getting out of bed. Sitting in a chair. Walking with help, then a walker, then a cane. Moving from the hospital to rehab and then home. Getting back behind the wheel of a car. Going back to work part-time and then full-time. These are seemingly little things and easily taken for granted—until you can't. Reclaiming each step is a breakthrough and cause for celebration.

Each step is a reason for expressing praise to God. As the writer of Hebrews conveyed, "*Let us, then, always offer praise to God as our sacrifice through Jesus, which is the offering presented by lips that confess him as Lord*" (Hebrews 13:15 GNT). He has been our constant companion through every leg of this excursion and the captain of the journey—responsible for the landmarks we have enjoyed along the way.

Last week, we recognized a great milestone. One year has passed since the sails were hoisted to cross the abyss of the unexpected turbulent seas. While she is far from fully recovered, there have been a host of small victories worth embracing. She tires easily. Sometimes her walking is very labored—the expected aftermath of two extensive hip surgeries. Yet she is able to reclaim most of life's experiences she enjoyed prior to the incident.

On Tuesday during her time in ICU, she *celebrated* her birthday. I brought gifts to the hospital and shared them with her when she was able. She received them with her characteristically gentle warm smile. She appeared to enjoy it as I read the opening chapter of the new book from one of her favorite authors.

Little did I know that she would recall nothing from the first week of her hospitalization—not the fall at home, not the two ambulance rides, and not the earrings for her birthday. Later, she would have to go back and read that first chapter for herself.

This year was different. A milestone. She received her birthday present with her characteristically warm gentle smile. She tried on this year's earrings, read the book, and enjoyed dinner out at the restaurant of her choice (a big step forward from a hospital tray!).

This foray into the stormy deep has taught us a great deal. Never take moments or people for granted. Trust God for each day. Appreciate the simple things. Display love openly. Gale-force winds and tempestuous seas will beset the routine of life eventually. Yet through it all, join the psalmist in faith declaring, *"But I trust in you, Lord; I say, 'You are my God.' My times are in your hands"* (Psalm 31:14–15 NIV).

CHAPTER 17

Course Corrections in the Aftermath

During our married lives, it became almost second nature. Date night has been and continues to be a nonnegotiable. Both Liz and I came out of dysfunctional homes. Communication at home was a very broken element of our parents' marriages.

Therefore, we were committed to never allow communication to be an issue between us. Other than our relationship with God, there was no more important relationship in our lives than the one with each other. We have chosen to keep each other the premier human connection in our lives. We are staunch believers in the directives of the scriptures which express, *"For this reason a man will leave his father and mother and be united to his wife, and the two will become one flesh"* (Ephesians 5:31 NIV).

Over our more than forty years of marriage, we have implemented practices to assure that *oneness* factor described our union. One of those has been a date night. It was determined that even in the lean years, time invested in keeping our relationship strong mandated a consistent time out. A weekly date night was an appointment kept. It didn't have to be elaborate or expensive. It was just focused time together. Many date nights were bowling with friends and a cheap pizza afterward. Even later in our marriage, it might consist of an inexpensive meal out and family shopping at Walmart. Yet we walked, talked, and stayed firmly connected.

A special date night opportunity arose when we knew that a movie release that interested us was coming. We'd save, prepare, and take in a film and refreshments (movie theater buttered popcorn was a must!). We were very selective in choosing a movie—money was normally a little tight, and we wanted to spend time in a fairly wholesome environment.

We had come to expect that sort of experience taking in one of the newly released animated classics by Disney. Over the years, we have enjoyed nearly everyone on the big screen. One of my recent favorites was the story of an island girl named Moana. The picture was bright and alluring. The story was engaging. The heroine sought to fulfill the longing inside her for the sea and to save the island of her people from a blight that was slowly killing it.

She set out on a great sea adventure. Ultimately, it took her to face the source of the problem. It was a volcanic creature named Te Kā. In their first encounter, Moana and her little vessel were thrown back by a giant wave in an angry backlash of Te Kā. She was cast far off and very much off course. It was nowhere near where she wanted to be. The loss in the encounter left the heroine feeling defeated, wondering about her destiny, and considering giving up on her quest.

In the aftermath of her harsh encounter, Moana had to come to grips with her setback and her feelings of failure. With the prompting of her grandmother, the heroine realized that sitting in the defeat of the moment was not her destiny. Lingering in her loss was not an option. She knew that she would have to try again.

Following this resurgence of purpose, she realized she had to go back and face the challenge which awaited her. It would require getting her bearings, calibrating her settings, and making course corrections in order to regroup from the stormy encounter with Te Kā. Moving onward was not an option. The mission ahead was far too crucial. The state of her future and the future of the ones she loved depended upon it. A new course was set, and a new course of action was adopted. While challenging, ultimately her adjustments and determination brought about a brighter day.

Thinking about that scene, I am reminded of how the power of a storm slamming into our lives can throw us way off course. Its blow can be demoralizing. It can rock the vessel of our experiences far from where we expected to be. Certainly, recovering from such a tsunami wave can leave the traveler unsure of where he is. It beckons to ask if there is reason to pursue the route that once had been charted. What will be demanded to advance once again?

There will always be course corrections necessary in the aftermath of a storm. Over the past year, while we have been able to record milestones of Liz's recovery, the torrent that had engulfed her physically was certainly a setback from the course on which she and I had been embarking. We have been making ongoing corrections in its aftermath.

They amount to an array of small things—as well as obvious larger ones. Once she was able to finally return home from the hospital and rehab facility, her care at home fell upon a novice rather than a team of health officials. I was given a crash course in giving intravenous antibiotic treatments. Each had to be given at specific times of day and over a rigid duration of time along with a regimen of oral medications.

I became a wound dress specialist. Each of her surgical areas had to be tended, covered, and waterproofed before helping into her shower seat. Then following a shower, they would have to be repacked and rebandaged.

Her nutrition was also crucial to her healing. Preparing nutritious and rounded meals along with wholesome snacks was on me. It's a good thing for her that I enjoy cooking and am proficient at it. Still, in the early days of her healing process, I remained engaged throughout the day with her care.

Nonetheless, I still had work to do. As a pastor, I had a faith family depending upon me to remain fresh in my own spiritual experience and in preparation for worship and teaching times. Our faith family was so gracious in allowing me to work from home and fully supporting my hands-on care for my wife.

Yet it required a course correction for me as I have always been a very present pastor. I find it rewarding to care for things at the church and in the lives of our people. Still, I had to learn to let others step up and to delegate. That is the way it is supposed to be anyway.

The ministry of the church is never intended to be a one-person operation but a collaboration of the giftedness of God's people serving together. As Peter wrote to the believers of his generation, *"God has given each of you some special abilities; be sure to use them to help each other, passing on to others God's many kinds of blessings"* (1 Peter 4:10 TLB).

There have continued to be course corrections as her healing has progressed. Yet, moving forward is crucial. In order to do so, we've had to adapt all while keeping the goal of living God's fullest clearly in view.

As I pen these thoughts, we are making our first trip to visit family in more than sixteen months. Florissant, Missouri, is over six hundred miles from our moms, brothers, sisters, and daughters who live in Michigan. Both of our moms are aging and not in stellar health. Few of the family have seen Liz since her health episode over a year ago. We felt it a priority to journey north to spend some time with them.

It is Thanksgiving Day, and we are preparing to visit with Liz's family over the annual feast. It has been a long season in the making. Still, even this trip has demanded adjustments.

I am one of those types who have no problem making a long drive. I would prefer to get in the car, go, and get there. It had been normal to drive the entire trip home with few stops along the way. Not so this time. Liz's condition will not allow it. Periodic stops have to be made so she can move around. If not, her repaired hip will become stiff and painful in the confines of the car. Flying is out of the discussion as well. The seating on planes is constricted. So what are the choices? We drive and stop as necessary. We make the trip in two days rather than one. Moving on to your desired destination is the goal even if the approach had to be adjusted.

I know that in the scope of things, these course corrections seem trivial. Change, however, is never easy. I have heard it said that the only human who really enjoys change is an infant in a dirty diaper—and even then, they've been known to put up a fight! Still, through the discomfort of resetting the trajectory of the days ahead, the end result must be kept in view.

I was drawn to a letter written by the great church leader named Paul to a group of Christ followers in his day. He explained to them the myriad of personal storms that battered his life—all while he was only being obedient to God. He wrote,

> I have been beaten the regulation thirty-nine stripes by the Jews five times. I have been beaten with rods three times. I have been stoned once. I have been shipwrecked three times. I have been twenty-four hours in the open sea. In my travels I have been in constant danger from rivers and floods, from bandits, from my own countrymen, and from pagans. I have faced danger in city streets, danger in the desert, danger on the high seas, danger among false Christians. I have known exhaustion, pain, long vigils, hunger and thirst, going without meals, cold and lack of clothing. (2 Corinthians 11:24–27 Phi)

Many of Paul's New Testament letters were written to congregations to help them—even while he was locked in a prison cell for his faith and work. He did not allow waves of hardship to keep him from the divine charge on his life. He simply adjusted and pressed on. He couldn't encourage them in person? Okay, he would instead write them letters and send ambassadors to deliver his correspondence. The outcome of his efforts is what was crucial.

He expounded on his endeavors at progress to another congregation. He explained,

> I keep working toward that day when I will finally be all that Christ saved me for and wants me to be. No, dear brothers, I am still not all I should be, but I am bringing all my energies to bear on this one thing: Forgetting the past and looking forward to what lies ahead, I strain to reach the end of the race and receive the prize for

which God is calling us up to heaven because of what Christ Jesus did for us. (Philippians 3:12–14 TLB)

The Thanksgiving dinner was wonderful. We were able to celebrate with Liz's family at the first home of Liz's nephew and his new wife. The season of storms necessitated some course corrections to get there. To have thrown up our hands and abandoned the destination when faced with the waves of trouble would have caused us to miss the blessing that awaited.

Has the torrent of trouble set you back? Has a typhoon-sized challenge sent the vessel of your life way off the course you had set for it? Check your compass. Review the travel plans established for you. Make course corrections and set sail for the God-conceived next leg of your journey. Hold tightly to the promises of the Divine Navigator who declared, "*I know what I'm doing. I have it all planned out—plans to take care of you, not abandon you, plans to give you the future you hope for*" (Jeremiah 29:11 Message).

CHAPTER 18

The Super Acts of the Slide Master

Ty was a hero. Oh, not that he ever donned spandex or a cape. He never did battle with a villain whose aspiration was world domination. Yet at least in the eyes of a few, his life radiated gallantry.

Ty is a young member of our church whose ministry role each Sunday is to oversee the visual components of the public worship celebration. He is the "slide master" of the congregational singing, making sure the song lyrics are presented for the congregation to sing along. His role continues in the time of the message. This pastor is a visual learner himself and does his best to keep the church family engaged with the teaching time using images and video components.

Ty takes his role seriously. He has been engrained with awareness of how vital his area of service is. Normally, he is joined in the tech center by a sound engineer. For his part, Ty's sidekick strives to assure quality audio for both the Sunday morning attendees and online viewership.

On a recent Sunday morning, the sound engineer's chair was vacated. With no available backup staff, Liz took over this important ministry. The tech center is elevated from the auditorium's main floor, so climbing up to attend this function was challenging. Nonetheless, she is pressing on in her recovery and doing what she is able. She stepped in and took a seat at the audio booth.

Ty has been schooled to keep himself free from distraction in order to assure visuals were cued properly. However, on this particular

Sunday, his cell phone vibrated with a message. The note announced the arrival of a package from Amazon being delivered to the front porch of his home.

He felt the need to apologetically explain to Liz the reason for the package's delivery. As his story unfolded, the moment of his heroic action came to light.

Ty is just in his early twenties and was hired about a year ago at a local hospital. He is serving in the patient transport department. The duty of those serving in this unit is to move patients throughout the hospital for various stages of their treatment.

Just like his approach to serving at the church, Ty understands applying himself while caring for patients at the hospital is essential. During a recent shift, he answered a call to the dialysis ward. There, he was to transport a patient to his next stop. As he arrived to receive his charge, he noticed there were a number of other patients waiting to be moved as well.

Completing his assigned transport, Ty returned to the dialysis department. One by one, he moved each waiting patient to their next stop. He had not been called to do it. He had not been assigned their care. He noticed their need and didn't hesitate to aid them.

One of the ward nurses took note of the young man's selfless endeavors. She was so struck by his willingness to serve that she honored him with a substantial Amazon gift card. Although it is steady work, transport employees are on the lower end of the pay scale in the hospital. She was determined to extend her appreciation for his quiet act of tending to others. A monetary reward seemed like an easy way to say "Thank you. Your act of kindness did not go unnoticed."

Ty was taken back by her generosity. Humbly, he resisted, but she wouldn't take "No" for an answer. Upon receiving the gift voucher, he ordered something that he had wanted but didn't really have the extra money to purchase.

He didn't fully grasp the extent of valor his simple unassuming actions had generated in the minds of others. As Liz listened to his account, she affirmed how important his deeds would have been to those he assisted. It had not been that long since she could recall being taken throughout that same facility for a barrage of tests she encountered over the eight weeks of her own hospitalization. Being on the receiving side of such care meant much.

She explained that when a person is waiting to be transported for a test or a procedure, the wait becomes wearisome. Apprehension rises. When it has been completed, the patient is tired, often uncomfortable, and longs to get back to their bed. The longer the wait, the greater the discomfort, fatigue, and the more negative the experience.

He might just see himself as pushing people in a wheelchair, gurney, or bed. Still, his portion of their care is far more vital than he understands. When a patient is tended to—even in this little way—it is a life-lifting intervention. That patient is in the center of a storm (their body is malfunctioning), filled with uncertainty (what will this test reveal?) and concern (what is coming next?). His quiet and confident intervention brings a bit of calm—if even for a short wheelchair ride.

He looked at Liz a bit stunned. He hadn't really seen himself in that light. His willingness to serve those people voluntarily—without assignment nor charge—made their day a little brighter. Ty told Liz he really had not given it much thought. He was just trying to do the "next right thing."

She smiled and encouraged him to continue. It mattered. It is the very thing that Christlike living generates. As Paul explained, *"And as the Spirit of the Lord works within us, we become more and more like him"* (2 Corinthians 3:18 TLB).

Consider how many times in the Gospels that Jesus reached out to the infirmed. Ponder the regularity in which Jesus brought a sense of compassion to those who had been shunned by society, scorned by humanity, and even disregarded by the very ones charged with representing God. Many of the records of the Gospel writers attest to Him seeing the crowds with compassion.

Doing the next right thing will not always result in a bonus, a pat on the back, or even recognition—at least here on earth. Jesus did the right thing every time, and He ended up on a cross! Still, His act of selflessness has been heroic to those who have received Him. Christ has changed their lives—life abundant and eternal!

A Christ follower's simple selfless acts for the benefit of others matter. They matter to the people who are on the receiving end. They matter as well to the one whose selfless sacrifice was made for our salvation. Jesus said, "*I'm telling the solemn truth: Whenever you did one of these things to someone overlooked or ignored, that was me—you did it to me*" (Matthew 25:40 Message).

Furthermore, your approach to others is a reflection of your relationship with God. As Paul explained to the believers of the first century,

> And don't just do the minimum that will get you by. Do your best. Work from the heart for your real Master, for God, confident that you'll get paid in full when you come into your inheritance. Keep in mind always that the ultimate Master you're serving is Christ. (Colossians 3:23–24 Message)

So rise up each morning and prepare to be a hero for someone by seeing a need, feeling the pain of those in need, and striving to address the situation. Demonstrate intrepid kindness. It's as easy as choosing to do the next right thing. No super suit nor cape required!

CHAPTER 19

Maritime Mementos

She sits back in the recliner. Her eyes are closed as she rests a bit from the events of a regular working day. I'm in the kitchen finishing preparation of supper. It is what I do. She keeps me around because I cook, clean, and make her laugh—not necessarily in that order.

I have taken seriously the role of providing healthy meals throughout the day to aid in her continued progress. Mornings kick off with a robust cup of coffee and a hot breakfast to follow. While she makes her way through breakfast, I turn to pack her a well-rounded lunch. Supper normally follows closely after she arrives home from work at five-fifteen.

Keeping on schedule is important. Serving in ministry often requires evenings back out for Bible studies, meetings, and music rehearsal. Now that Liz is able, she wants to be involved with me. Supper following serving is not best, so we press to finish before heading back out.

My roles at home have needed to expand as a result of Liz's illness. For example, our laundry area is in the basement. She cannot easily navigate the basement stairs. (However, we did find she could a few weeks ago as a tornado warning sounded!) Stair climbing of any sort is really a challenge on her surgically reconstructed hip and leg. It is one of the many reminders of braving a collision course with a storm.

You might call them maritime mementos. Paint slashed exposing the wood below. Tears in the sails that once propelled you. Metal marred, dented, and bent. Seams exposed. All evidence of the ravages of the storm.

One of my favorite films of all time was the classic *Raiders of the Lost Ark*. It created the iconic character Dr. Henry "Indiana" Jones. After the adventuresome quest for the lost Ark of the Covenant, Jones's love interest, Marian, notes how the years' quests have taken their toll on him. "You're not the man I knew ten years ago," Marian observed. Jones responded, "It's not the years, honey, it's the mileage."

Navigating through torrents in a dinghy can leave lasting reminders of the stressful undertaking. When slapped by whitecaps in the middle of the sea, flooded to capacity, near swamping, and pummeled by the gale-force winds of devastating circumstance, the vessel of your life will inevitably be marred. You will have to determine what you will do with those reminders.

Each storm, in each life, will leave its own unique imprint. They can be physical, emotional, relational, and even spiritual. I have witnessed them all on the other side of the foul weather front in our lives.

As I survey the aftermath of my wife's altercation with her own, there are many evident vestiges. Physically, there is an extensive scar on her hip as evidence of two surgeries. A four-footed cane is her constant companion. She tires easily. Cool or damp weather causes her repaired joint to cramp up and ache. Sleep can be a challenge.

The storm damage left behind necessitates careful choices when going places. It means she sits in the car when there are no amigo carts at the grocery store, and I do the shopping. There can be no long drives in our convertible (it sits low to the ground and getting out becomes problematic). She's had to entrust me with the laundry (stairs) and housework (she can no longer push a vacuum).

Those and more weigh heavily on her emotionally as well. It is disheartening to her that she is so limited. Furthermore, her progress has slowed a great deal, and there is no assurance that her full mobility will return. Patience is stretched thin. When she gets distressed, it is reassuring to sit down and just recount how far she has come.

Spiritually, many other issues are visible. Questions pound the psyche like hail before a tornado. Why her? She is a good woman, a loving mother, and my partner in life. She has served the Lord faithfully at my side for more than three decades. Why now? Was there something that I overlooked or that I failed to do?

All of those questions are above my pay grade. Asking them really strives to achieve nothing. Linger there in that place and bitterness blankets the heart like a dense morning fog.

Those questions drag one down as he views the damage a torrent brings. Yet repeatedly, God uplifts the hearts of His faithful children to a different view. He bolsters the soul regardless of the aftermath. Paul explained to the believers in Rome, *"We know that in everything God works for the good of those who love him. They are the people he called, because that was his plan"* (Romans 8:28 NCV).

Admittedly, not everything is good. Life can deliver the power of an unsuspected hurricane. Yet in the midst of the pummeling winds and drenching cloudbursts, God has assured us that He is leading us through it. He is up to the challenge even when we feel that we are not. He is teaching us more about Himself and how He will use these heart-trembling moments for a cause that could not be seen in the deluge.

Yes, Liz still displays the evidence of the storm. The sails have been battered. Bow and stern are a bit worse for the wear. Would I want to enter those headwinds again? No. I much prefer smooth sailing.

Still, it is clear that God's hand has been leading toward good even when we could only see threatening clouds and rough seas. I have been the beneficiary of praying people. Not just a few. Literally, from coast to coast, there have been people talking to God about us. There have been God moments that have been direct interventions to the course we were on.

In these months of havoc, I have witnessed God at work, not just for the good in my wife's healing but in shaping me. Realizing how near I was to losing Liz, God has set ablaze a deep love for her in me. We have long had a very tight bond, but I will cherish every moment I'm allotted with her.

Through these turbulent days, I was also drawn to see the power of authentic Christian community at work. It is a book-of-Acts quality—people praying and a faith family lifting your burden, carrying your weight with you. Since that time, we have put a high premium into the organization of a "Congregational Care Team." The ministry role of this team (at the moment led by three women who have been ministry wives) assures that each participant in our church family experiences that genuine community in a variety of manners. This exercise of community is too vital to leave to chance.

Liz and I have a story to tell. Our experiences were the precursor to this journal. Writing it began as personally therapeutic. It was a way for me to unpack my feelings and center my prayer thoughts.

Continuing this endeavor was an avenue to encourage other people who find themselves in the fearful moments when they are walloped by the unexpected and uncontrollable. Our story may help them as they sail through theirs. As Paul wrote,

> What a wonderful God we have—he is the Father of our Lord Jesus Christ, the source of every mercy, and the one who so wonderfully comforts and strengthens us in our hardships and trials. And why does he do this? So that when others are troubled, needing our sympathy and encouragement, we can pass on to them this same help and comfort God has given us. (2 Corinthians 1:3–4 TLB)

Life is a bit different now. It is not hard to see the mementos of the melee that marked our lives. God has been with us through it all. If we understand that God will take those things and shape them for good, I can live with a scar or two.

CHAPTER 20

The Big Deal in Little Things

You'd think after the apex of the torrent's threat had been weathered, it wouldn't have seemed like much. I mean, waves were not swamping the boat. The rain was not pelting those maneuvering the craft. There was no gale-force wind shredding the sails that could propel you toward the shoreline. This is nothing like the enveloping darkness and tumultuous menacing squall that is long behind.

So why does it get under one's skin when they are encountered? Why should it consume so much of the mind? They are nothing like the storm that has already passed—but little things. They are not much more than paltry annoyances. They are the slivers in your finger, misplaced keys, forgotten passwords, and walking into another room with purpose only to forget the reason why when you get there.

We make a big deal out of little things. I've had one of those weeks and have found myself moaning about such annoyances. A few days ago, I tweaked my back so I'm moving a little more slowly and much more gingerly. I had an appointment with the eye doctor for some laser surgery to clear up an issue. I've gone through it before, so there was nothing to raise concern.

Then in the chair, the doctor said he could not do the procedure, and it would require something more extensive. He scheduled it for two days later. I would be down just a couple of days to recover. Later that night, I received a contact from a parishioner to tell me she had COVID. She was one of the leads from the hospitality team at church and the second lead ministry family to be confirmed this week. Under an abundance of caution, we will be shifting to just an online presentation this week. There is so much I need to get done and am being inhibited by *stuff*. I know, after all God has brought our family through this year, I'm making a big deal out of little things.

In the epic dialog of Job in the Old Testament, his experience was one of severe heartache. A thunderous and ominous storm front collided with the vessel of his life. The impact was devastating. He had lived a virtuous life, one of which God had even noted, yet it did not spare him the ravages of the unforeseen typhoon that crashed in on what had been clear sailing.

What was so impressive was Job's support network as he braved the heartache of all he encountered. The compassion of his dear wife was moving. *"His wife said to him, 'Are you still maintaining your integrity? Curse God and die!"* (Job 2:9 NIV).

Then there were his three good friends who stopped by to see him through this period of personal grief. Their efforts began so nobly.

> When Job's three friends, Eliphaz the Temanite, Bildad the Shuhite and Zophar the Naamathite, heard about all the troubles that had come upon him, they set out from their homes and met together by agreement to go and sympathize with him and comfort him. When they saw him from a distance, they could hardly recognize him; they began to weep aloud, and they tore their robes and sprinkled dust on their heads. Then they sat on the ground with him for seven days and seven nights. No one said a word to him, because they saw how great his suffering was. (Job 2:11–13 NIV)

Nevertheless, when the silence was broken, so was their compassion. Each pointed a finger at Job explaining that it must have been something that Job had done to bring on such tragedy. It must have been Job had been involved in a hidden sin that had provoked God's wrath and judgment. If Job only owned up to his failures, things could be restored. Well, Job was guilty of nothing, and the mayhem of the storm which had invaded his tranquility was not God's hand of vindication.

Sailing on life's sea sometimes crosses paths with turbulent weather. In like manner, there is an element of living that can be a series of annoyances—nicks, scrapes, miscues, interpersonal disruptions, late-night wrong number phone calls, overzealous work associates, long checkout lines, and the like. They are not at all as intense nor threatening as the power of a storm front that broadsides without warning. Yet don't they tend to weigh you down, take the pep out of your step, and disquiet your mind?

As Job was confronting the *insight* of the companions who were there to comfort, he made an interesting observation. *"Those who are at ease have contempt for misfortune"* (Job 12:5 NIV). He was calling out those who had been spared the devastation he had experienced. Still, at my first reading of the verse, I saw a whole other side to it. Those who are enjoying smooth sailing get perturbed at anything that makes waves.

My mind repeatedly is turned to the Hebrew nation during the leadership of Moses. God freed them from the heavy burden of Egyptian slavery. With their backs against the wall of the Red Sea, God parted the waters for them to cross over on the dry ground and then eliminated the pursuant Egyptian armies in a tidal wave. Over and again, God intervened to clear the way when the clouds of trials were billowing all around them. His presence was clearly evident with each of their steps.

Nevertheless, at the first sign of a little annoyance, they began to murmur as if life itself was meant to be irritant-free. They foolishly pined for the "good old days" when they were slaves. Can't you hear them whining about those daily bothers? "Oh, really? Manna—again tonight?" "Are we there yet?" "God must not love us to let us go through every day like this."

They made a big deal out of the little things. They forgot that the God who had provided in the storm was there to support them through the irritation. The God who had freed them from the oppression under which they were living was leading them to a homeland of promise. The trip would have some relatively small annoyances. As Job observed, *"We are all human beings. Our life is short and full of trouble"* (Job 14:1 ERV). However, the same God who demonstrated His faithfulness in the big things, who provided what they needed, held them up in battle, and used the voyage to hone them into a people with purpose—a nation and holy ambassadors to the world (Genesis 12).

God never promised that the way would be free of those things that sometimes chafe His people, but He did pledge them a purpose, power, provision, and destination "flowing with milk and honey." The Apostle Paul discussed the reality of such an annoyance as he penned a letter to the believers in Corinth. It was a "thorn in the flesh."

> I was given a thorn in my flesh, a messenger of Satan, to torment me. Three times I pleaded with the Lord to take it away from me. But he said to me, "My grace is sufficient for you, for my power is made perfect in weakness." Therefore I will boast all the more gladly about my weaknesses, so that Christ's power may rest on me. That is why, for Christ's sake, I delight in weaknesses, in insults, in hardships, in persecutions, in difficulties. For when I am weak, then I am strong. (2 Corinthians 12:7–10 NIV)

So I will, too, rely on God's grace being sufficient over this series of little annoyances. Right now, I'm feeling a bit weak. The big deal in these little things is not me handling it but allowing Him to do it through me.

CHAPTER 21

A Rising Tide in a Cyclone

When braving a torrential onslaught during an excursion, what is most likely to surface in a person? When the stress of challenging circumstances and unexpected trouble fall like sheets of rain, what will show itself most readily? As you consider the outbursts of some of the very human examples found in the pages of the scriptures, maybe you and I can see a bit of ourselves.

As has been referenced frequently here, Jesus's disciples did what they were conditioned to do. Fishermen know the routine of manning a craft confronting the teeth of a storm. They just bury themselves in their craft. They put their experience into high gear. Working harder—even expertly—aside from trusting Jesus still leaves the boat tattered and sinking.

The Old Testament prophet Elijah comes to mind. He had been on the top of his game. Standing alone for the God of the Hebrews, Elijah had silenced a horde of four hundred fifty priests of the idol Baal. It was a great victory that rallied the Hebrew people to the God of their faith.

God revealed Himself for this generation of the nation to see. A lengthy famine was then broken. The rain was restored. It was a glorious day, and everyone was pleased—everyone that is but Queen Jezebel.

She was a "Baalite." The defeated and destroyed prophets of Baal infuriated her. While the gentle rains refreshed the parched land, a storm of rage gathered in Jezebel's heart. The Bible historian records, "*So Jezebel sent a messenger to Elijah and said, 'I swear that by this time tomorrow, you will be just as dead as those prophets. If I don't succeed, may the gods do the same or worse to me*" (1 Kings 19:2 ERV).

The barometer reading had shifted. Elijah was now in the direct path of the deluge of the queen's anger. So how did the reality of the storm front impact the prophet who had seen the mighty hand of God bring down fire from heaven at Elijah's prayerful request?

You know the story. When trouble rained down and the threat of retribution from the queen blew in, Elijah ran and hid. "*When Elijah saw how things were, he ran for dear life to Beersheba, far in the south of Judah. He left his young servant there and then went on into the desert another day's journey*" (1 Kings 19:3–4 Message).

Four hundred and fifty opposing theologians, no problem. God's got this. A blood-thirsty queen? I'd better hit the road and lay low until the storm passes.

That's not the only response to trouble that surfaced in the once-valiant and victorious Elijah. Not only did he run and hide from the pressure confronting him, but he began to moan and languish feeling sorry for himself.

He offered up his well-rehearsed grievance to God. "*Lord God Almighty, I have always served you—you alone. But the people of Israel have broken their covenant with you, torn down your altars, and killed all your prophets. I am the only one left—and they are trying to kill me!*" (1 Kings 19:10 GNT).

Yet Elijah's assessment of the cyclone bearing down on him was not what he believed it to be. God spoke to the prophet and revealed that his appraisal was jaded by self-pity. It also left out vital insights. Earthquakes, violent winds, and the roaring flames that raised the human pulse held no consequence to the still, small voice of God who had everything well in hand.

So when the teeth of trial confront you, what is your default? What reaction rises to the surface from within you? Bury yourself in work? Turn and run to avoid the stress of trouble? Sit down and tearfully lament how unfair life is and even blame God for turning a deafened ear to your situation?

Let me offer yet another example to consider. There is a fellow mentioned in the biblical record who encountered the mother of all storms at sea. Not literally, but certainly, his life's voyage could have equated it. His name is Job.

Job was said to be a man who honored God with all of his life. He had worked hard and amassed an impressive portfolio. He had been a good father to his children. His sons and daughters had a cohesive family relationship and enjoyed one another's company. It was an example of righteous living.

One might believe that such a person as Job and his family might be shielded from the sorts of trouble that so often invades human tranquility. These were models of godly people—hardworking, loving family, revering God with all their living.

Nevertheless, with the suddenness of a Kansas tornado, violent storms in the form of human calamity drop on the unexpecting. In a matter of hours, Job's family was devastated by such a pattern of wicked weather. His wealth in the form of his herds was eradicated. His children all were killed during one of their family gatherings by a freak storm that leveled the home on top of them.

How did Job respond? What arose in him in the face of this devastating hour? Did he dive into work to restore his wealth? Did he flee and put his stress behind him? Did he grumble in depression and point a finger at God? None of the above.

The Bible reveals much about the heart of Job. Some of Job's counter to the incoming wave of ruin bombarding him demonstrated both his humanity and his deep connection with God. The writer of Job's encounters with many storms (the aforementioned are just the beginning) physically, relationally, and economically reveals a response not often associated with hardship.

The writer explains, "*When Job heard this, he got up and tore his robe and shaved his head to show how sad he was*" (Job 1:20a NCV). It is natural to be dismayed at the times of sorrow, brokenness, and despair that can invade our lives on this side of eternity. Showing sadness when things are troubling is not a lack of control but a natural expression. Jesus, Himself, wept. Job had lost his economic security for which he had invested himself and lost his children. Finances and family were wiped out. Mourning was expected.

Yet the writer gave his readers the other side of Job's response. It was a rising tide in the face of a cyclone. From deep within, expressed even as his tears fell, Job lifted up his heart to God. *"Then he bowed down to the ground to worship God"* (Job 1:20b NCV).

Worship God? It is uplifting God not only in spite of, but in the face of, mourning and uncertainty. It wasn't that God had caused Job's misery. Invading torrents are simply a part of the sailor's expectations when navigating the seas of life. As Peter told his fellow believers, *"Dear friends, don't be bewildered or surprised when you go through the fiery trials ahead, for this is no strange, unusual thing that is going to happen to you"* (1 Peter 4:12 TLB).

While swamped in the reality of his heartbreak, Job worshiped God. In God, peace in the storm could be found. In God, the confidence in navigating the storm was assured even though at the moment tears flooded his eyes. God could be counted on to even bring good out of the devastation of the occasion. As Paul assured the people of faith in his generation, *"We know that in everything God works for the good of those who love him"* (Romans 8:28 NCV). We may not see it at the moment. We may not understand the picture as God sees it. Yet we can trust that while not everything that happens in our lives is good, God can bring good through it.

I've heard people say, "God must have done it for a reason." I don't exactly see it that way. There are things that come into the life of the individual—stormy seasons, occasions that rock one's being that one would not consider *good*. Not everything is good that comes our way.

Yet even in those circumstances, God can bring good out of them. The good may be in molding our character (Romans 5:3–4). Those rough waters that we have made our way through may be used to enable us to assist another whose boat is floundering on those same seas (2 Corinthians 1:4). We can be sure that when trouble finds its way into our experience, God is not on the sideline but is actively setting things in motion to bring good out of it. Worship is a fitting response.

The concluding verse of the chapter adds, "*In spite of everything that had happened, Job did not sin by blaming God*" (Job 1:22 GNT). No, even in the heartbreak and loss, Job determined to trust God's hand regardless of the blows he took due to circumstances. "*I will continue to trust God even if he kills me*" (Job 13:15 ERV).

It is my prayer that during the seasons that steal tranquility and rock life's vessel, I will be drawn to worship God. As the rains come and the winds blow, God hasn't changed. His gentle hands can wipe my tears, bolster my heart, and assure my shaken confidence. His wisdom can be trusted to bring good out of the challenge being encountered—whether it is good in me, good through me, both and more.

Sail On!

When I was younger (oh, my, much younger!), there was a trend-setting Gospel group that had a long list of inspiring songs. Having originated as an edgy men's quartet, The Imperials set the pace for a very different flavor of Christian music. While still featuring smooth harmonies, they produced music that captured a new generation of listeners.

During the height of their influence on Christian music, they recorded such memorable songs as "Praise the Lord" (featuring newcomer Russ Taff), "Bread on the Water," "The Eagle Song," and "The Trumpet of Jesus." Another was a song including the lyrics with which I want to close this journal of thoughts. It was a simple song entitled, "Sail On."

Life is a series of seasons with both smooth sailing and turbulent encounters that raise anxiety. Yet, remember as you make your way toward that final destination, Jesus is in the boat. He is capable and trustworthy even when the rains fall, the winds blow, and the waves are high. As Jesus told His disciples, *I have told you all this so that you may find your peace in me. You will find trouble in the world—but, never lose heart, I have conquered the world!* (John 16:33 Phi). So, friends, sail on!

> Sail on
> When the water gets high
> Sail on
> When the wind starts to die

Sail on
It's just a matter of minutes
'Til His ship comes to get us
And we'll all get in it
Cast up your sails
And let the wind blow
Jesus will never let your ship lose control
Just keep your compass set on the Son
And He'll guide you safely to His beautiful home
("Sail On," lyrics by Chris Christian ©1977
      Curb Word Music)

ABOUT THE AUTHOR

Mike Warren is a husband and father of two adult daughters. He and his wife, Elizabeth, began serving in various local church ministries in the early years of their married lives. For the past thirty-five years, they have been in full-time Christian service. Mike currently serves as senior pastor in the greater St. Louis, Missouri, area. He earned his bachelor's degree in religious studies and master's degree in teaching from Oakland City University.